SAVE TAX DOLLARS

REDUCE COSTS; MERGE AND ORGANIZE GOVERNMENTS

TOM, THE TWENTY-FIRST CENTURY RADICAL

iUniverse, Inc.
New York Bloomington

Save Tax Dollars
Reduce Costs; Merge and Organize Governments

iUniverse books may be ordered through booksellers or by contacting:

iUniverse
1663 Liberty Drive
Bloomington, IN 47403
www.iuniverse.com
1-800-Authors (1-800-288-4677)

Because of the dynamic nature of the Internet, any Web addresses or links contained in this book may have changed since publication and may no longer be valid. The views expressed in this work are solely those of the author and do not necessarily reflect the views of the publisher, and the publisher hereby disclaims any responsibility for them.

ISBN: 978-1-4502-5279-9 (sc)
ISBN: 978-1-4502-5281-2 (ebk)

Library of Congress Control Number: 2010912172

Printed in the United States of America

iUniverse rev. date: 9/21/2010

AUTHOR'S NOTE

The author has studied decision-making processes and their relationship to organization. With proper organization of the federal, state, county, and local governments, there will be tremendous savings in taxpayer dollars. The author has relied on Internet search engines to confirm the facts that support the conclusions contained in this book. Therefore, the facts are readily available to the reader.

Acknowlogements

The author thanks his wife, Eunice, for putting up with him for sixty-five years. A special thanks to iUniverse Publishers, especially. As always the editorial help is greatly appreciated and is invaluable. Thanks for the major editorial help.

FOREWARD

The present governments in the United States were established in the eighteenth century. Now that we are in the twenty-first century, it is time for reorganization of the federal government and improvements in the organization of our state, county, and local governments. The First Constitutional Congress established the Congress, an Office of the President, and the Supreme Court. Powers were granted to each of the three branches of the federal government. The organization of the state, county, and local governments was not mentioned in the Constitution.

From the data presented in this book, it is obvious that the lack of proper organization of state and county governments has added a very large amount of government overhead and resulted in inefficient use of taxpayer dollars. Federal, state, county, and local governments have not followed tenets used in the business world to establish efficiency and effectiveness.

The words of the U.S. Constitution are not set in stone. The Constitution allows amendments. The federal budget has a large deficit, and the federal debt is in the trillion-dollar range. Most taxpayers believe the federal government is dysfunctional.

The lack of a standard requirement for population of the States has resulted in large variations in state populations. This population difference has led to an oversized Congress. The members of Congress have various and widely different agendas.

Today, only five states do not have a budget deficit. There are major differences in the number of county governments within a state. Within these various counties, there are large and small local governments. All of these governments—state, county, and local—add overhead to the budgets.

A merger could decrease overhead spending and provide a tax base that meets budget demands. Increasing the number of taxpayers for each of these governments would reduce the individual taxpayer's burden. Government borders need to be set in order to establish efficient and effective governments.

CHAPTER 1

REASONS WHY TAXPAYERS AND VOTERS SHOULD FOLLOW THE ACTIONS OF THE COLONIES

Since the eighteenth century Americans have always been in charge of their destiny. The citizens have come together to fight adversity. We have seen the American spirit in times of war and peace. The great Depression, the Manhattan Project, cure of Polio, and the NASA program are all examples of America's success. America can reorganize the federal government, and organize state, county and local governments. This effort will save billions and over time trillions of tax dollars.

In the eighteenth century, the British wanted to punish the colonies for the Boston Tea Party, so they put in place tax laws to produce social changes in the colonies. The laws increased dissatisfaction in the colonies and led to the Declaration of Independence. This error in decision-making judgments by the British government was most likely due to the distance of the point of the decision from those affected by the decision. Distance from the individuals affected by a decision is only one factor. Another factor is cultural and social understanding of the individuals affected by the decision.

Another error made by the British was the use of tax laws to bring about a change in society. Tax dollars should be used to fund the government; thus, it is improper to use tax laws to bring about changes in society. When a government uses taxes improperly, the laws complicate the tax codes and make them very difficult to enforce.

These same British mistakes are being made by Washington today. The tax codes are complicated by the use of tax laws by the president and Congress to bring about changes in society. It is time for a taxpayers' Declaration of Independence.

As was stated in the original Declaration of Independence:

> We hold these truths to be self-evident, that all men are created equal, that they are endowed by their Creator with certain unalienable Rights, that among these are Life, Liberty and the pursuit of Happiness. — That to secure these rights, Governments are instituted among Men, deriving their just powers from the consent of the governed, — That whenever any Form of Government becomes destructive of these ends, it is the Right of the People to alter or to abolish it, and to institute new Government, laying its foundation on such principles and organizing its

powers in such form, as to them shall
seem most likely to effect their Safety and
Happiness.

Borders are established by people, and these borders
can be changed for the benefit of the people. In Europe
the borders of each country are established by ethnic
and language differences. In the United States, English is
the official language, and our melting-pot society allows
borders to be drawn for other reasons. These reasons will
be discussed in detail.

Do the citizens of the United States feel "safe and
happy" today? Discussions and polls have shown that
about 75 percent of the citizens are dissatisfied with the
performance of Congress. After a period in office, recent
presidents have had less than 50 percent approval of their
performance from the citizens. Today we have government
"by the people" for the benefit of the officeholder and not
for the benefit "of the people."

Daily we hear cries for "term limits." Others call for
voting incumbents out of office. The two political parties
will not work for the good of the country. State and local
governments do not have the funds to provide proper
services for their citizens. It seems like every day we hear
or read about the state, county, and local governments'
struggles to fund important programs. Individual citizens
have lost their jobs and their homes. Certainly one cannot
call this situation "safe and happy."

It is time for the people to demand major changes in
their governments. To get agreement among the citizens,
both Democrats and Republicans, that the country is in
desperate financial trouble is like getting agreement that
the ocean is blue.

Yet with all the calls for change, one does not hear the cry for a well-organized and structured constitutional convention. The major charge to such a convention should be to organize the governments.

Citizens need to have decision making nearer to the people affected by the decision. With proper organization, there could be a reduction in budget cost. Spending, especially on government overhead, could be far less than what is currently spent for federal, state, county, and local government.

When one thinks of patriotism, is he thinking of others or is he thinking of himself? President Obama says patriotism is faith in other Americans. Some Americans have performed in a manner that is very deserving of one's faith, while others have not. John F. Kennedy said it best: "Ask not what your country can do for you. Rather, ask what you can do for your country." Americans are the sum of America's parts. As a patriot works for the good of the country, he is working to improve America for all Americans. Both the federal government and society seem to have lost their faith in each other and in other Americans.

It is apparent that the citizens have lost their faith, especially their faith in government officeholders. We need to get all governments and society working for the improvement of the safety and happiness of the citizens. With proper organization of our governments for effectiveness and efficiency, we can again have faith in our governments and the individuals in our society.

ORGANIZING BY MERGER TO DECREASE OVERHEAD AND IMPROVE THE TAX BASE

The First Constitutional Congress established a Senate with two senators from each state. The House of Representatives was established with one representative for every thirty thousand individuals. The Congress did not establish size or population values for statehood and did not establish a number for counties in a state, nor did Congress establish a population value for counties. Thus, size and the population of the states and the number and population of the counties are vastly different among the existing fifty states. The lack of organization of these governments increases overhead spending for governments and costs the taxpayers millions or possibly billions of dollars.

Facts learned in corporate organization classes govern corporate organization. The first is the fact that corporate income must be sufficient to meet the expenses. Thus, when a corporation does not meet expenses, it should consider a merger. The income from the increased market share can meet the new corporate expenses. Market share should be large enough to provide a corporate profit.

The second fact is that when the corporation becomes large and diverse, it needs to be divided into profit centers that can be managed. The current federal government has passed the point where many of its functions need to be turned over to the states.

Because of size and complexity, many of the current functions of the federal government are dysfunctional. There are competing functions in the federal government and too many layers of conflicting responsibilities. This is very obvious in the Congress. A very important fact is that transferring federal functions to the state level will bring decision-making nearer to the points affected by the decision.

Federal, state, and local governments have not followed these business facts that assist corporate organization. A merger has two advantages: first, it can increase market share and income; and second, it can reduce overhead expenses. Dividing a large corporation into smaller profit centers reduces the complexity of decision-making and brings the decision-making nearer to the point of operation. Generally, this can be done without increasing overhead expenses.

Tax income for governments is like market share for corporations. The market share should be large enough to provide a profit, and the tax base should be large enough to provide a government surplus. Currently, federal, state, county, and local governments almost all have a deficit.

Raising taxes is not an option. The loss of wealth with the recession prevents increasing taxes. Corporate taxes cannot be increased because the corporations will move operations out of the country to decrease overhead. Governments should, instead, consider reducing overhead. This can be accomplished by merger of existing governments. Federal government functions need to be divided among the states. This is similar to corporations dividing functions into profit centers. The data clearly support reducing overhead for federal, state, county, and local governments. It is definitely time for a change.

While the freedoms granted by the Constitution are timeless, the management of federal, state, and local governments is time dependent. When the Constitution was ratified, there were thirteen states, and the population was just slightly more than one million citizens. Virginia had twice the population of any of the other states. The federal budget was well under two million dollars.

Today, Congress is composed of 535 individuals, the budget is so large the Government Accounting Office cannot keep up with the spending, and the population is approaching four hundred million citizens in fifty states. While the current population of the United States of America is 308,687,437, using a population figure of four hundred million seems reasonable since considerable time will be required to form and carry out a Constitutional convention. We all know the population is increasing at a very rapid rate.

Most citizens agree that spending is out of control and Congress is not making an effort to control spending. There needs to be an effort to reduce the current debt and the budget. The interest on the national debt increases the budget cost. The federal government has become excessively involved in corporate business. We are seeing more and more federal laws that affect individuals and corporations. Excessive taxes are driving jobs overseas. When laws are made that affect individuals and businesses, they should be made near those who are affected by the laws—not in Washington.

Currently, thirty-five states are suing the federal government because the government's actions have adversely affected the states' budgets. It takes thirty-eight states' votes in order to have a Constitutional convention. A Constitutional convention could study and advise on new organization and management of federal, state, county, and local governments. While a convention could bring about desirable changes in our method of government, the size and complexity of the problem will require considerable effort on the part of the individuals who are members of the convention.

Using a Constitutional convention to bring about the needed changes may be considered revolutionary. Evolution brings about change for survival, while revolution brings about chaos.

It is time taxpayers and voters took an interest in their governments' finances. We would not need a Constitutional convention to bring about changes in state, county and local governments. It is better when changes are made by evolution. These slower changes are less disruptive of ongoing functions. The taxpayers and voters can bring about mergers of their governments. These evolutionary changes cause less chaos, but can be extremely effective at reducing the cost of governments.

CHAPTER 2

LACK OF ORGANIZATION OF CURRENT GOVERNMENTS AS SEEN IN STATE POPULATION AND NUMBER OF COUNTIES' FIGURES

It becomes very obvious from the following figures that there is an urgent need for merger of both state governments and county governments. There is a complete lack of organization in the states and counties. This lack of organization is costing taxpayers possibly billions of dollars. With the current condition of the budgets it is necessary to improve efficiency at all levels of government. There are several internet sites that give population data for states and counties with in a state. The number of counties in a state is also included in several sites. These data have slight differences. The slight differences do not affect the conclusions present in this book.

Alabama: The population of Alabama is 4,500,752. There are sixty-seven counties in the state. The median population of the sixty-seven counties is 67,185. This is about the population of a small city. The state has a general funds budget of 1.5 billion dollars, and it is expecting a major shortfall in 2010.

Alaska: This state is different from all the other states. Alaska has a population of only 648,818 people, but it still has sixteen boroughs. Thus, the median population for each borough is 40,551. In addition to the sixteen boroughs, Alaska has many smaller area governments called counties. It is a good thing Alaska has money from the sale of oil, because they are wasting a lot of money on local government.

Arizona: The population of Arizona is 6,500,180. Almost half the population resides in Maricopa County, which has a population of 3,072,149. The state has fifteen counties. Therefore, 3,428,031 people reside in the remaining fourteen counties. If 3,072,149 people can be governed by one county government, why does it take fourteen counties to govern 3,428,031 people?

Arkansas: The population of Arkansas is 2,855,390. The state has seventy-five counties. The median population of the seventy-five counties is only 38.886 people. Many of the counties in Arkansas have fewer than ten thousand people. The smallest county is Calhoun County, which has only 5,435 people.

California: The population of California is 36,756,666. This is the largest population of all the states in the union. With this large population, California has fifty-eight counties. This is seventeen counties fewer than Arkansas. With just five states considered so far, we see that the current organization of the fifty states is very random; very little thought has gone into state and county organization.

Colorado: The population of Colorado is 4,939,456. The state has sixty-four counties. Thus, the median population for the sixty-four counties is 77,804. The population of two counties, Denver and Arapahoe, make up more than a million people of the almost five million people in the state. On the other hand, Baca County has only 3,834 people and appears to be losing population. A county was added in 1998, Broomfield. Instead of merging, it appears Colorado is increasing administrative overhead.

Connecticut: The current population of Connecticut is 3,518,285. There are eight counties in the state. Arizona requires fourteen counties to govern this many people.

Delaware: This is another small state, with a population of 885,969. Yet Delaware has two senators, the same number as the state of California. Naturally, with only three counties, the number of representatives is very few. This is a great place for merger. Maryland and Delaware should consider merger. This would reduce the number of senators by two and increase the number of representatives for Maryland/Delaware.

Florida: The population of Florida is 18,537,969. There are sixty-seven counties in the state. With half the population of California, Florida has more county governments. Until the recent recession, Florida was one of the fastest-growing states in the union. Florida should consider a merger of counties and a discontinuation of local governments. These mergers would provide much-needed capital for services and projects in the state. State officials, including the governor, are complaining about state budget problems, but they ignore the benefit of a merger to reduce overhead costs.

Georgia: This state is an excellent example of too many county governments. While the population of the state is 9,829,211, there are 159 counties. Several counties have fewer than two or three thousand people. While Fulton County has 1,033,756, Glascock has only 2,801 people. If one county is operating with a population of one million, why not have all counties have at least one million people and reduce the number of local governments? The taxpayers should appreciate the savings by these mergers.

Hawaii: Hawaii and Alaska are different from the other forty-eight states. Hawaii has a population of 1,295,178 and has four counties. These counties are on the various islands. Alaska has a population of only 648,818 and has sixteen boroughs. Hawaii operates with just one board of education. Think of the dollars we would have for student education if each state had one superintendent of education and one board of education. Small offices located around the state could handle contracts and other business affairs.

Idaho: The population of Idaho is 1,545,801, with forty-four county governments. What do you think of this state and local government organization?

Illinois: This is a very interesting state in terms of lack of thought and organization of its government. The state population is 12,910,409. Cook County has a population of 5,256,037. There are 102 counties. Pope County has just 3,991 people, and Stark County has 6,019. With the government of Chicago and Cook County as an example, it seems taxpayers should have realized they were paying too much for county and local government. With this example of Cook County and Chicago there for all to see, it seems action would be taken to better organize the government. Maybe they never heard of a merger.

Indiana: The population of Indiana is 6,423,113, with ninety-two counties. Once again, the borders of Randolph County were changed to form new counties in 1998. Spending tax funds on government overhead could not have been a factor in this government decision.

Iowa: The population of Iowa is 3,067,856, with ninety-seven counties. With only half the population of Indiana, Iowa has more county governments.

Kansas: The population of Kansas is 2,818,747, with 105 counties. These three states—Indiana, Iowa, and Kansas—are good examples of the lack of planning that has gone into state and county government. We are now in the twenty-first century, and the United States was established in the late eighteenth century. After all these years, one would think either the federal government or state governments would have realized governments need thoughtful organization. We have state governors who meet regularly. What do they work on at these meetings? It is time taxpayers asked this question.

Kentucky: The population of the state of Kentucky is 4,314,113. The state has 120 counties. This is the third largest number of county governments among the fifty states. Kentucky recognized that many of its counties did not have a sufficient tax base to support the needed services, but the people voted to keep their county borders. Is it any wonder why the mountain areas have a high poverty level?

Louisiana: The population of Louisiana is 4,492,076. There are sixty counties in the state. Kentucky has about the same population as Louisiana, but Kentucky has twice the number of counties. The Kentucky state budget is 456 million dollars, while the Louisiana state budget is 341 million. This is a difference of 115 million dollars. While the federal government deals in billions and trillions of dollars, 115 million dollars would eliminate the debt of many states.

Maine: The population of Maine is 1,318,301, and the state has sixteen counties. Cities with this population operate with one government.

Maryland: The population of Maryland is 5,699,478, and the state has twenty-three counties. Look at the difference between Maryland and Massachusetts.

Massachusetts: The population of Massachusetts is 6,593,587. There are six counties in the state. The size of the state in area seems to be more of a factor in deciding the number of counties than the wise use of taxpayer dollars.

Michigan: The population of Michigan is 9,969,727, and there are eighty-three counties. Michigan is one of the states hardest hit by the 2008 recession, with a large gap between income and expenses.

Minnesota: The population of Minnesota is 5,266,214, and the number of counties is eighty-seven.

Mississippi: The population of Mississippi is 2,951,996, with eighty-two county governments. The budgets of Minnesota and Mississippi differ by only nineteen million dollars. Mississippi ranks last in the fifty states in many areas, such as education and social services. Saving tax dollars by mergers could help the budget.

Missouri: The population of Missouri is 5,987,580, and there are 114 counties in the state. While the population of Minnesota and Missouri are not very different, the state budgets differ by 353 million dollars. The differences in the state budgets are evidence for improving efficiency by organization.

Montana: The state of Montana is one of the states with a population of fewer than one million. The population is 935,670, and there are fifty-four county governments. Neighboring states of North and South Dakota each have a population of less than one million. These small states contribute two senators each. While this representation is supposed to be offset by the number of representatives, the U.S. Senate remains a very important governing body. This is an area of the country where merger should be considered.

Nebraska: The population of Nebraska is 1,756,787, and there are ninety-three counties. While pride in state and county governments must be considered, it pales in comparison to the savings in tax dollars that could be obtained with consideration of government efficiency. Mergers of states in this area of the country would reduce the cost of government for state taxpayers and also reduce the cost of the federal government by reducing the number of senators.

Nevada: The population of Nevada is 2,414,807, and there are sixteen counties.

New Hampshire: The population of New Hampshire is 1,309,946, and the state has ten counties.

New Jersey: The New Jersey population is 8,717,925, and there are twenty-one counties. With New York City and New York State as examples, one would think New Jersey would realize their governments are not operating efficiently.

New Mexico: The population is 1,928,384, and there are thirty-three counties in New Mexico. When New Mexico and Arizona were admitted to the Union, tax base was not a consideration. Merger of these two states would reduce overhead and improve the tax base.

New York: The population of the state of New York is 19,254,630, and there are fifty-seven counties. New York City has a population similar to the population of New Jersey. The population of New York City is 8,214,426. New York State could benefit from merger of county and local governments.

North Carolina: The population of North Carolina is 8,683,242, and the state has one hundred counties, twice the number of counties in New York State. While New Jersey operates with an excessive number of counties at twenty-one, North Carolina has one hundred. The population of New Jersey and North Carolina add up to be about the same as New York City.

North Dakota: This is one of the smallest populations of all the states: 636,673. The average population of a U.S. Representative district is 650,000. The number of counties in North Dakota is fifty-three. New York State operates with fifty-seven counties with a population of 19,254,630.

Ohio: The population is 11,464,042, and there are eighty-eight counties.

Oklahoma: The population of Oklahoma is 3,547,884 with seventy-seven counties.

Oregon: Oregon has a population of 3,641,056, with thirty-six counties. While the population of Oklahoma and Oregon are nearly the same, Oklahoma has twice as many county governments that require funding from the tax dollars.

Pennsylvania: The population is 12,429,616, and there are sixty-six county governments.

Rhode Island: Rhode Island is one of the smallest states in area and has a small population for an eastern state. The population is 1,076,189, and there are six counties. Does this suggest to you that merger of states should be considered?

South Carolina: South Carolina is a small state in terms of area; but like most of the original thirteen colonies, the population is fairly large. The population of South Carolina is 4,255,083, and there are forty-six county governments. South Carolina has just eleven counties less than New York State, with a population of 19,254,630. The author hopes that by now you can see the need for merger.

South Dakota: Both South Dakota and North Dakota have very small populations. The population of South Dakota is 775,933, and there are sixty-four county governments. Thus, with fewer than one and a half million people, North and South Dakota require 117 county governments. This is an excellent example of where merger would reduce overhead for both state and federal government.

Tennessee: Tennessee has a population of 5,962,956, and there are ninety-three counties.

Texas: Texas and California are both large in area and have large populations. The population of Texas is 22,859,968, and there are 254 counties. Harris County has the largest population. There are 3,984,349 people in Harris County, with 2,144,491 people living in the city of Houston.

Utah: The population of Utah is 2,469,585, and there are twenty-nine counties.

Vermont: The population of Vermont is 623,050, and there are fourteen counties. When you compare Vermont with North and South Dakota, you can see the need for merger of county governments. While merger of state governments would be a larger problem, these data support the suggested merger of county governments. Merger of the small population states with other states would make a remarkable contribution to saving tax dollars.

Virginia: Virginia was the largest of the original thirteen states. Today the population of Virginia is 7,567,465, and there are ninety-five county governments in the state.

Washington: The population of Washington is 6,287,759, and there are thirty-nine counties.

West Virginia: The population of West Virginia is 1,816,856, and there are fifty-five county governments.

Wisconsin: The population of Wisconsin is 5,536,201, and there are seventy-two counties.

Wyoming: The population of Wyoming is less than the population of either North or South Dakota. The population of Wyoming is 509,294, and there are twenty-three county governments in the state. While the average population required for a representative in Congress is 650,000, Wyoming has one representative and naturally two senators. Is this really one person one vote?

The differences in the populations of the states led the First Constitutional Congress to decide on a bicameral congress, meaning there would be two legislative chambers. While this might have been a solution to a problem in the eighteenth century, the bicameral congress has become dysfunctional. There are too many members with widely different agendas, and the needs of the governed are very different.

A bicameral congress adds to the confusion, as well as the dysfunction and cost, of federal government. While a bicameral congress was suppose to aid the one man one vote concept, it has not achieved its objective. The Senate is composed of more senators from states with smaller populations. Ten small states control 20 percent of the Senate. While the larger states have more representatives, the 435-member House dilutes the effectiveness of each representative.

The number of members in the House of Representatives increases the cost of the federal government substantially. California has a population of more than thirty-six million and has two senators. It would take the population of the twenty smallest states to equal the population of California. It is obvious we need to reduce the complexity of the federal government that has developed since the time of the First Constitutional Congress. Many of the current federal functions need to be state functions.

While we need to clarify the wording of the freedoms established by the first amendment to the Constitution, they must continue to be the framework of our government's relationship with the country's society and individual citizens.

Now that we have seen the lack of organization in state and county governments, it is obvious that there is a need for the following three changes: (1) Improve the use of tax dollars. (2) Bring decision-making near to the point affected by the decision. (3) Reduce the size and cost of our governments. These changes are very necessary to providing efficiency and effective government. The process of merger brings decision-making nearer to the people affected. Mergers are very important to the efficiency of government and reduce the cost of government overhead.

Example Changes that a Constitutional Convention Could Bring About

The following example is one method for reducing the size of federal government and reducing the cost of state, county, and local government. This example is given to promote discussion and action by current government entities.

The reader will find the following example very radical. We become satisfied with the status of our environment even if the environment is not effective and is inefficient. But with thought and effort, voters can bring about the needed improvements in our governments.

The following example is presented to show what can be accomplished by moving federal functions to state functions. This brings decision making nearer to the people affected by the decision. In addition, organizing state, county, and local governments can improve government efficiency by decreasing the cost of government overhead and improving the tax base.

The Constitutional congress will be faced with the problem of deciding on the number of states. The government could be composed of any number of states. The tax base is the major concern. Having large population states with Regions with populations near four million would provide an adequate tax base. Moving federal functions is important, and reduces the cost of federal government.

The financial condition of the federal, state, and many county and local governments shows the need for radical changes in our governments. It is easy to become complacent with the existing status. We fail to look for methods of change. But the current dysfunction, excessive cost, and debt of governments require we consider radical changes at all levels of government. The business merger provides a decision process for voters and taxpayers to consider.

> 1. With a population of four hundred million, we could have states of twenty million each. That would be twenty individual states. Thus, we would have a merger of states. This would reduce government overhead.

> 2. The federal congress should be composed of one hundred senators. One senator from each region. The Constitutional Congress should consider whether the senators should be elected by voters or appointed by the legislature of the individual states. If the senators were appointed, they would

serve at the pleasure of the individual state legislatures.

The representatives in the House are elected by districts within a state. Therefore, the representative is elected by a very small percentage of the total population. The current population of a district is six hundred fifty thousand. This representative can become a powerful member of Congress and have a profound effect on citizens from all fifty states. Both the Speaker of the House, Nancy Pelosi, and the House Republican Leader, John Boehner, are good examples of individuals elected by a very small percentage of the population.

The average district that elects a representative is six hundred fifty thousand people. The winner of an election to Congress usually receives slightly more than 50 percent of the total votes. With twenty states of almost equal population, there would be no need for a House of Representatives. We could say good-bye to the dysfunctional bicameral congress.

3. The senators could elect a president, who would be responsible for the executive management of the country. Since the duties of the president would be to manage the programs designed by the senators, the president would serve at the pleasure of the senators. This appointment

process would place the major power of the federal government in the hands of the members of the Senate.

4. The twenty states would each be divided into five regions. This would provide one hundred regions. The many county and local governments would be merged into a region. This would represent a merger of county and local government to reduce the overhead in state government. Each region would have a population of near four million.

The state government would be composed of a legislature. The members of the legislature would be elected by the voters of the regions. Each region would elect two legislators. The legislators would appoint a governor. The governor would serve as the chairman of the legislature.

5. The voters of each region would elect a council. The council would be composed of nine representatives.

6. The region's council would appoint a mayor, who would be responsible for the management of services to the people of the region. The reduction of elected officials would require adequate numbers of staff positions for each official. This would provide adequate data generation and analysis. However, after briefings from

their staffs, the officials would negotiate before voting on a plan of action.

7. Any individual who meets the criteria set by the legislature could run for any elected office. The criteria should include the number of names required on a petition submitted by the candidate to the election committee. Selection of the election committee would be a function of the legislature.

Another suggested organization would be to eliminate the twenty state governments and have only a federal government and one hundred regional governments. The populations of the regions would be near four million. Currently twenty-seven states have populations near or less than four million. This organization could increase the number of federal senators. If each region had one senator, the federal government would have one hundred senators. The population of four million would not have a tax base large enough to support the move of federal functions to state functions. The federal government would remain large.

The author is not trying to dictate actions of a Constitutional convention. The examples are given to provide the decisions process. While the taxpayers will benefit greatly from the savings, the author would also like to benefit from the savings in tax dollars.

Currently, the size and organization of states is not dependent on the tax base meeting the state's expenses. We have excessive county and local governments. The federal government is trying to manage states that have many differences.

We have states that are agricultural, others that are industrial, and others that depend on tourism and other forms of business. The major source of income and the need for services differ greatly among the states. With the proposed twenty individual states, decision-making in major areas of need will be near the area affected by the decision. However, since the individual state's size would be smaller than the current federal government, the decision-making process would be much less complicated.

The boundaries for the twenty states should be set in place so that each individual state will have a tax base to provide sufficient funds to cover the state's budget and provide a surplus fund. County and local governments need considerable help. Like the state government, the proposed regional governments should have taxing authority and a tax base sufficient to meet budget demands.

There should be a constitutional requirement that all governments have yearly balanced budgets. The budget should include a surplus fund. Since there is always a variation in income to expenses, the surplus is necessary to take care of this difference. When the surplus funds are used, they should be replaced in a timely fashion.

Most city and town governments are very dependent on state and federal funds. The expense and the tax base do not match. Changes in size and management of the county and local governments can reduce government cost and provide considerable funds for taxpayer services.

The establishment of twenty individual states represents corporate structure changes made when a board of executives can no longer control the corporation and decides to divide the corporation into profit centers. Moving federal functions to state functions is part of the change. This reduces the federal cost of overhead and brings decision making nearer to those affected by the decision.

Naturally, there could be fifty states with two regions in each state. Fifty states and 100 senators is familiar. This reduces the population of the states. Fifty states and one hundred regional governments add additional governments above the proposed twenty states and one hundred regional governments.

THE DATA USED TO SUPPORT THE EXAMPLE

The author knows these changes are very radical. However, when one considers that the changes could decrease the cost of governments by billions and over time trillions of dollars, they are worth consideration. After the wealth loss caused by the recession, the decrease in cost of governments is very necessary.

A twenty-five-mile hike starts with a single step. While there is need of a Constitutional convention to bring about thorough reorganization of the current governments, we can bring about change by merger: (1) Merger of local governments with local governments. (2) Merger of local governments with county governments. (3) Merger of county governments with county governments. These changes within a given state could substantially reduce government overhead.

A Constitutional convention should be charged with evaluating various forms of change to our current government. The purpose of the convention would be to devise an effective and efficient government. The work of the convention will be extensive. The members of the convention should have good decision-making skills. The members cannot be like many committee members, who begin thinking about the committee at the meeting room door and forget about committee business when they leave the room.

The Constitutional convention will need an excellent chairperson. The chairperson should be able to make assignments to members that can be handled with sufficient effort. These assignments would provide the convention with important information and data.

The above paragraphs show that the author has watched the current Congress and is very concerned with the dysfunction of Congress and other decision-making functions of the federal government.

If a Constitutional convention was to propose the suggested changes, it would take a major effort on the part of the voters to have the changes approved. Therefore, we need to take a hard look at the data that support these changes.

The reader might think that twenty million people are a very large population for an individual state. The estimated population of New York State was 19,490,297 in 2008. New York City is the sixteenth-largest city in the world. The estimated population of New York City was 8,214,426 in 2008. The proposed population of the five regions in the twenty individual states is four million, which is less than half the population of New York City.

In fact, the population of New York City is greater than the population of most current states. This information should make each of us realize we are spending our tax dollars on unnecessary government. Florida has an estimated population of 18,325,340, with fifty-seven county governments. That makes the population of even the larger Florida counties less than one fourth the population of New York City.

When you consider that approximately twenty of the existing states do not have the required four million people to make up a region under the proposed plan, and five others just barely meet the population requirement, it is easy to see that currently we are spending too much money on government.

Since twenty-seven of the existing states have populations near or less than four million, it might be a better idea to drop the state governments and have one hundred regional governments.

Four states are above or near the required twenty million proposed for state population. The existence of these states assures us that the requirement of a population of twenty million is not out of range. But the regional populations of four million are nearer to the existing organization.

The reduction in federal functions and the movement of these operations to the twenty states will cause a substantial increase in the state's budget. Transfer of the current funds spent on these functions and the reduction in county and local governments will further increase the funds available to both the budgets of the states and the five regions of each of these states. The savings in reduced overhead spending, caused by the current lack of organization, should reduce government cost and save taxpayer dollars.

Texas is one of the states that has a population of more than the required twenty million for the proposed states. In fact, Harris County in Texas has almost enough population to qualify for regional status. Now consider the fact that Texas has 254 counties. This does not include the local governments that require funding.

While the state budget of Texas would not necessarily change, the organization of the county and local government into regional governments would provide substantial funds for the Texas state functions. There should also be funds that are currently used by the federal government. Considering the current population of Texas, it could support six regional governments.

New York State has a population of more than nineteen million. Thus, it too would qualify for state status in the proposed program. New York City would have sufficient population to make up two regions in the state government. This information provides evidence to support the proposed government reorganization.

Since New York City is currently operated by one government body, it is obvious that two regional governments would be acceptable government. These state and local governments that are very large would benefit the least from the proposed changes. Their governments are already serving a large population. But the existence of these governments that serve large populations support the value of meager in governments in other parts of the country.

New York State would gain from the reduction of county and local governments in the parts of the state other than New York City. All of the large states could benefit from a merger of county and local governments. It is obvious we are spending excessive overhead funds for our governments.

As stated above, when Kentucky attempted to reduce the number of county governments, pride in the area caused voters to resist changes. It should be remembered that pride goes before a fall. Social areas and government areas exist for different reasons. Everyone should take pride in the area where they live. But pride in a social area is an emotion. Governments' borders exist for management reasons. The borders for government need to be established for tax funding and management reasons. The tax base should be sufficient to fund efficient government management. Efficiency is defined as excellent management with the lowest tax cost to the individual taxpayers.

If the proposed example should be activated, the one man one vote principle would become a reality. It is obvious from the differences in the populations of the states and the number of counties in a state, that the effects of these factors on the one man one vote concept have not been considered.

Each state has two senators, while the House of Representatives is supposed to make up for the population difference. The first Constitutional convention was not prepared for the population growth that has occurred since the eighteenth century. This growth has added to the ineffectiveness of the federal government. The 435 representatives dilute the authority of each individual member.

CHAPTER 3

THE NEED FOR EDUCATIONAL CHANGES

While this book has spent much time on organization of the governments, the functions of government deserve examination to find methods of improving efficiency and effectiveness.

We have learned that states cannot meet their budgets. A careful look at one government function can provide a good example for studying other functions. Education is an excellent example to study, because it is extremely important and very costly.

Once again, looking for mergers would help. There would be a substantial increase in the budgets of the individual states to carry out programs, projects, and services if county and local governments were merged. Likewise, merger in functions like education could reduce overhead. Do we need all the boards of education that we have in the states? Hawaii has a population of 1,283,178. Hawaii has only one school district, operated by one school board. While the school system is divided among the islands of the state, there is only one district.

This is a good example for other states to consider. The proposed regions should have only one school district. In this twenty-first century, school districts, colleges, and universities need to evaluate their curriculum and educational methods. Functions like student acceptance and other management functions could be merged among the colleges and universities. Such mergers would reduce costly overhead spending.

The current revolution in multimedia and electronics has provided excellent tools to improve educational methods. For example, the Kindle can download books from anywhere. Students with Kindles would not have to buy printed books. Thus, the cost of the books would be considerably less. Finding information in the books contained in a Kindle is very simple. The student searches by words or phrases, similar to looking up information in a book's index. However, the search is done by typing and submitting a word or phrase. Just think of students carrying a Kindle and not lugging five to ten large textbooks.

Well, the use of Kindles in education must be a good idea. I thought this would be an original idea when I wrote the above paragraph. Just before I returned this manuscript to the publisher after the original review, a local high school announced they are buying Kindles for the entire student body. Their reasons for the purchase are the same as those given above.

We are seeing more online classes at all levels of education. The use of electronic devices in schools better prepares students for the twenty-first century. Maybe standing up and talking at students has become a thing of the last century. Everywhere we go, we see people with something stuck in their ear. Think of the learning that could occur if students and others were listening to study material instead of rap music.

The iPhone has put knowledge at our fingertips. The knowledge that is available on the Internet extends from bits of information to complete courses. Now it is time for high schools and universities to teach students how to use the information that is at their fingertips. With excessive information, students need to know things like how to make decisions where there are multiple choices and multiple applications for each choice. Yes, this is a simple task if you know the method.

IT IS PAST TIME TO ACCOMPLISH THE TASK

At this time when greed by citizens and financial institutions has created a major financial crisis, it is time we consider every avenue for reducing cost and improving efficiency. The amount of dollars lost by this greed is discussed later.

Think about how much money we would save by acting to bring about the proposed changes in the size and cost of federal, state, county, and local governments. Twenty individual states with near equal population would reduce the size and complexity of the federal government. While the final Constitution would be the result of the work of the Constitutional Committee, the following information is given as further support of moving government nearer to the area governed. The states should govern health, energy, education, housing, parks and recreation, commerce, and other legislation currently within the control of the states.

The federal government would control defense, with support from the states. In addition, the federal government would be responsible for the State Department, interstate transportation, and functions now carried out by the Department of the Treasury. Wall Street has control of the money, but voters have control of the ballot box.

Voters must get organized and demand that Main Street take back the government from Wall Street. Demanding merger of current governments at the federal, state, county, and local levels will bring control back to the voters. This is an example of dividing a large corporation into profit centers, reducing the complexity of government and improving efficiency. Reducing the number of states, counties, and local governments is an example of mergers.

The individual states will need an adequate tax base, just as companies need an adequate market share. A major problem for the members of the Constitutional convention will be establishing working relationships and areas of responsibility between federal and state governments. The author is sure that by now you realize that the changes in government suggested here will reduce the number of government jobs.

These massive layoffs are very disturbing, especially with our attempts to recover from the recession. However, if we substantially decrease the tax cost to our citizens, these dollars will become available for improving individual lifestyle. We should see a substantial increase in consumer spending. Therefore, we should see growth in the corporate workforce. The increase in consumerism paid for with cash means an increase in our tax base. The reduction in government jobs and the increase in corporate jobs are very desirable. We all agree that it is better to have individuals paying their share of the tax burden than it is having individuals contributing to the tax burden.

It is easy to see that to accomplish the changes required by the example will take a very long period of time. However, taxpayers and voters do not have to wait a long time to begin reducing the cost of governments. When corporations face a deficit, they begin to reduce overhead spending. Generally, the first attempt to save costs is to turn to reducing work hours for individual employees.

However, with our current crises, we need greater savings. Management looks for mergers within the corporation and ways to downsize staff. One of the first places management looks for reduction of overhead is in middle management. State and county governments are part of middle management in governments. Long before we have the reduction in overhead proposed in the example, we can have reductions in government management cost by merging county and local governments.

Reducing local government cost by merging local governments with county government is easily possible. We have seen actions by cities to bring unincorporated areas into the city. At the insistence of the voters and taxpayers, these mergers could occur quickly.

With the loss of wealth and the increasing government deficits, it is obvious that we need to make changes to improve efficiency. Naturally, these changes in government need to be done in an orderly manner. After review and discussion, we should have laws that direct these changes in government. Voters need to insist that officeholders begin this process.

With the electronic media available today, we need to have organization of the taxpayers and the voters. The Tea Party is one example. The author is not a blogger, but bloggers are needed. The country needs to bring individuals into organizations that have a sufficient number of voters to bring about change.

CHAPTER 4

HISTORY REPEATS ITSELF

While division of power between the states and the federal government may seem to be arbitrary, it has been debated since the early meetings of the Continental Congress (1774). The Federalists and the states' rights groups debated which government should have power.

The First Constitutional Congress was dominated by the Federalists. The First Constitutional convention was obviously more interested in the Congress than other branches of government. Article one Section 1 makes this point clear: "All legislative power herein granted will be vested in a Congress of the United States, which will consist of a Senate and House of Representatives." Article one of the Constitution deals with the number of members of both houses of government and the powers of the Congress.

While some colonies were in favor of strong individual state governments, the Federalists wanted more power for the central or federal government. Under the Articles of

Confederation, the states retained sovereignty over all governmental functions not specifically relinquished to the central government. The First Constitutional Congress "corrected" the Articles of Confederation by establishing a strong federal government. It must be remembered that at this time there were thirteen states and the population of the country was near one million. Organizing the government with one major government site was a wise idea. This saved the tax dollars that would have been spent in the thirteen states.

At the birth of this new nation, we had an excellent example of authority existing at some distance from those affected by the laws of the authority. The colonies sent delegates to both the First and Second Continental Congress. The British Parliament had passed the Coercive Acts, also known as the Intolerable Acts. The British Parliament, separated by so many miles and time from the colonies, thought the acts would punish Massachusetts and Boston for the Tea Party, as well as restore British authority and restore loyalty by all the colonies. Most colonists believed the acts were a violation of their natural rights, and this led to the Revolutionary War.

The government organized by the first attempts of the Continental Congress points out how long we have struggled with the method of government. For example, from the beginning we have had problems with representation. The Articles of Confederation gave equal representation to each state. The states with the largest population were expected to provide the major portion of the funds to support the central government. Naturally, this was a point of contention with the larger states.

After the failure of the Articles of Confederation, the Constitutional convention set up a government with one house with each state having equal representation, the Senate, and another house having representation based on state population. It is interesting that the house having representation based on population was given major budget consideration. All money bills had to originate in the House.

Thus, the convention decided on a bicameral congress. Several nations currently have a bicameral congress. But these nations are smaller in area and population than the United States. In bicameral governments, the Senate, or upper house, is thought to be the wiser chamber.

The Constitutional convention decided that each state would have two senators, who were elected by the state legislature. The Senate was seen as a stabilizing force. In a number of instances, we see that the framers thought the senators were better prepared to lead since they were elected by the state legislature. They considered election by the people to be a method that would elect fewer wise individuals. Therefore, rather than one house of Congress, we need two: one to look out for errors of the lower house.

With the growth of the United States, we have seen an ever-increasing number of congressmen. While we have maintained two senators from each state, we have seen the number of states grow from thirteen to fifty. Some states have a population much less than a million and other states have a population of twenty million or more, yet each state has two senators.

Because of the explosion of the population, we have seen much larger growth in the number of representatives in the House. The Congress realized the problems with this growth and on March 4, 1913, Law 62-5 locked the House size at 435 House members. Naturally this has reduced individual representation. At this time, the average population of a district that elects a representative is six hundred fifty thousand. When the population reaches four hundred million, each district will have a population of nearly one million.

There was a debate during the Constitutional Congress about the number of members of the House of Representatives. George Washington favored one representative for every thirty thousand people. James Madison agreed that increasing the number of representatives was not a good thing. He believed that sixty or seventy men might be more properly trusted with a given degree of power than six or seven. But Madison did not believe that six or seven hundred would be a better answer.

In 1790 each member of the House represented thirty thousand people. In 1890 each member of the House represented 151,912 people. By 1990 the number represented had increased to five hundred ninety thousand; and in 2010 the number of people represented by a member of the House has increased to approximately six hundred fifty thousand. When the number of people represented was thirty thousand, each person had a much better knowledge of their representative's character. In a group of thirty thousand individuals, it is much easier to become well-known; however, in a group of six hundred fifty thousand individuals, the representative is not well-known to the voters.

While it was generally believed that senators elected by the state legislatures were better prepared to lead and could serve as protection for the states, the one hundred senators of today cannot be expected to serve this function because there is a great difference in state size and population.

Since smaller states are more numerous, they have the largest number of senators and therefore the largest number of votes. Setting the population of the states to approximately the same number of citizens and maintaining a single house of congress seems more likely to simplify decision making and reduce bickering. All of the examples given for consideration give the power back to the people.

A major problem with current district structure for the House of Representatives is gerrymandering of the district. If politicians spent as much time on government efficiency as they do on politics, we would have a much better government. The party in power changes the border in order to increase the number of votes in favor of the party in power.

We have a change in the borders of the representative districts every ten years. Changing the individual state and the region borders every ten years should be acceptable. A suitable arrangement would be to set the state's borders at the time of the ten-year census, so that each state and region would have a tax base that would meet expenses and provide a surplus. The taxpayers are paying for the census—we should use the data.

As suggested earlier, the Congress would consist of one house, the Senate. Think about the elimination of the cost of the House of Representatives. There would be a reduction in election cost as well. If the funds spent on election were spent on improving society everyone would benefit.

Having elections of senators be national elections rather than state-controlled elections would have the effect of maintaining a Senate body with a national interest. Such an election process would remove control from the people of the individual states. It seems better to have one senator elected or appointed by each of the one hundred regions. The Seventeenth Amendment set appointment of senators by the state legislatures. In the 1913–14 term, Congress spent much time on its organization, and the selection of senators became a state popular vote process.

Such election could give an individual state more representation. While the operations of the Senate would be national, each state would have two senators with an interest in the welfare of their state. The Constitutional Congress will be faced with deciding on the method of selection of federal senators and state offices.

Why should we have a president who is appointed by the Senate and serves at the pleasure of the Senate? It was thought by both Continental Congresses that individuals who were elected by the state legislatures would be wiser and more experienced than individuals elected by a popular vote. The popular vote generally does not consider the candidate's ability to govern. The election is a popularity contest. The large amounts of money spent by special interest groups contribute to the candidate's popularity.

When the Senate chooses a president, the Senate would conduct a background review and judge the candidate's ability to carry out the duties of the presidency. If their decision turned out poor, then the president would be removed by a vote of the Senate. The term of the appointed president would be five years. After five years, the Senate should review the service of the president. The individual could be reappointed or replaced. These appointments instead of having elections would reduce spending on election processes. Everyone knows the high cost to the candidates for elections. Most of these funds come from donations. It would be much better for the citizens if these donations were used to support social programs.

Law Enforcement and Responsibility Are Very Important for Safety

The laws of the states and the federal government are only as good as the enforcement of the laws. We have heard that traffic safety depends on engineering, education, and enforcement. In our complex society, gaining respect for the laws and responsibility for obeying the laws become extremely important.

Currently, citizens are more afraid of crime in their neighborhood than they are of terrorist attacks. The Constitutional Congress will be faced with the task of providing a federal and state system to enforce the laws. Remember that government is supposed to be for the safety and happiness of the citizens.

No one should be above the laws of the land. Currently, the elected president appoints the federal attorney general. This system puts the attorney general under the direction of the president. It seems it would be much better if the attorney general were under the direction of the citizens. A new government system having an attorney general proposed by the senators and approved by a majority of the governors of the states would place the attorney general under the control of the citizens.

The attorney general is in charge of the federal police force, the FBI. The nation needs a strong federal police force with all the technology available to solve crimes. This federal function needs to be well funded because it is responsible for the safety of the citizens.

When one considers law enforcement, one needs to consider the court system. The federal Supreme Court serves a major function in today's government. Currently the judges of the Supreme Court are appointed by the president and confirmed by Congress. In the proposed changes to the current government, the senators should propose the judges, and the governors of the individual states should have approval. The proposed judge would need a majority vote of the states' governors.

The federal Supreme Court would be responsible for constitutional law and settling interstate cases. Since the laws and the enforcement of the laws are so important, the states and the regions need a law enforcement system similar to the proposed federal system. The regions will need their own police system and court system. The states should have a police system and a court system. The state's Supreme Court would serve the function now served by the state's Supreme Court.

These examples change the equality among the three current branches of government: Congress, the executive branch, and the Supreme Court. The granting of great autonomy to the states lessens the need for the checks and balances now in place. Since the states are going to provide the funds for federal operations, they should have control over the federal government.

Term limits are often discussed by citizens. Many state governments have term limits for governors, and the U.S. president is also subject to term limits. Bringing government near to the governed makes term limits less important. The voters can remove the governor and members of the state legislature. Senators can be removed by the state legislatures at any time. We have recall votes. The Constitutional convention may want to consider an article that deals with recall votes. Currently, a large segment of the population is dissatisfied with the Congress. But we generally vote the same people into office. Albert Einstein once said, "Insanity is doing the same thing over and over again and expecting different results."

CHAPTER 5

NOW IS THE TIME FOR CHANGE

Thomas Jefferson said that every generation needs its revolution. Revolution brings about chaos. Evolution brings about change for survival. The civil rights granted by the Constitution were discussed and debated in the coffee houses of England and taught by pamphlets in the colonies for years. It is beyond a doubt that the civil rights are timeless and must be preserved.

However, the government established by the Constitution needs change. The forefathers realized the need for change and established a method for amendment of the Constitution. It seems likely that if the framers of the Constitution were here today, they would once again raise the need for a revolution.

But modern intelligence demands evolution as a method of change to bring about survival. After more than two hundred years since the Constitution was ratified, we have seen sufficient growth in size and population to support the need for another Constitutional convention.

The current federal, state, county, and local governments all have large debts and budget deficits. These conditions call for evolutionary changes for survival.

Congress has a very low approval rating. Every four years we have political conventions, where devoted members of parties elect a candidate for president. The devoted members of the two major parties represent about 60 percent of the citizens. This procedure leaves about 40 percent of the citizens with the problem of whom to vote for. As a result, many citizens do not vote *for* a candidate; they vote against the one they like the least.

Once a person is elected to Congress, they seem to forget that the government is a government "of the people, by the people, for the people." It is interesting to note that South Carolina has a population of nearly four million citizens. The population of the United States is nearly four hundred million citizens. Thus, the citizens of South Carolina represent about 1 percent of the population of the United States. Republican Senator James DeMint was elected to the U.S. Senate by Republican Party members in South Carolina. He was elected to the Senate by less than 1 percent of the nation's population. During a recent senatorial vote, Senator DeMint and one other senator voted against seating Hilary Clinton as Secretary of State. President Obama appointed Hilary Clinton to the position of Secretary of State. President Obama received more than 50 percent of the national vote, while Senator DeMint received votes from about 0.5 percent of the total voters in the United States. Does this really support government of the people, by the people, for the people? Or is this government with political party bickering?

With the current near 50 percent popularity of President Obama and the low approval rating of the Congress, President Obama is supported by a larger percent of the people. Political bickering is another cause for the dysfunction of the government. By the time laws are passed, the 24/7 news has most people uninformed as a result of the reporting of untruths and half truths during the bickering. Frequently we find out too late that the talking heads have not read a proposed bill. By supporting the bickering the networks increases the program ratings.

Surely, when a person is elected to the Senate, he should have the support of more than 0.5 percent of the people. In 1786, when the Constitution was ratified, each of the twenty-six senators represented the views of about 13 percent of the people. However, states like Virginia, which had the largest population, had senators who represented a much larger percentage of the population.

The current two-major-party system causes problems with elections. Senators and representatives are constantly concerned with reelection. They must please their party to be nominated for another term. Recently we have seen the results of this with the election of Senator Joseph Lieberman. While he lost the support of his party, he was elected as an independent senator. This indicates the Democratic Party did not represent the will of the state's voters.

The current method of government has led to a major financial crisis. Even the so-called fiscal conservatives are spending money that the nation does not have. They are eager to place pork projects in much-needed congressional bills. Recent events have shown that Main Street has lost to Wall Street.

The reader should not think that problems with government have only occurred recently. The colonists were not the first to have problems with government. The following quote is attributed to Cicero in 55 BC: "The budget should be balanced, the Treasury should be refilled, public debt should be reduced, the arrogance of officialdom should be tempered and controlled, and the assistance to foreign lands should be curtailed lest Rome become bankrupt." We all know about the fall of Rome. Survival of our position in the world is dependent on substantial improvement in our financial situation. People must be given the opportunity to work, instead of living on public assistance.

As stated earlier, it is time we discussed the effects of the recession on net wealth. According to reports seen on the Internet, this loss of value could exceed thirty-two trillion dollars. With the current number of unemployed or under employed; the income loss removes more than a trillion dollars from circulation. The reduction in the cost of real estate has contributed to this loss. Foreclosures, short sales of real estate, and personal bankruptcies have contributed to a lowering of individual net worth. Reports state that consumer credit card and other debts could contribute as much as fourteen trillion dollars to this loss. While recently we have seen some improvement in investment value, the loss in individual net worth experienced in the recession is far from recovery.

Now for the good news: the loss of excessive consumerism is seen as a good thing by economists reporting on the Internet. Buying expensive items on credit is generally necessary to support the economy. However, considerable thought must be given to the buyer's budget and the ability to make at least monthly payments to reduce the interest payments. The large debt owed by consumers contributed substantially to the recession.

Economists' reports on the Internet have suggested that many of them saw the coming of the recession. They have pointed out the need for a substantial reduction in government spending. The cost of the federal deficit must be reduced. While there is a need for a tax increase to balance the federal budget, the loss of value of individual net worth does not support a tax increase. Therefore, governments are left with only one option: decrease spending by the governments.

What Can Be Accomplished with Effort by the Voters

While the freedoms granted by the Constitution are timeless, the management and government of the United States are affected by time, population, and budget.

The first and second constitutional conventions were established to organize federal government and provide an effective government for the thirteen states, with a population of slightly more than one million citizens. The national budget was well under two million dollars. The debt of the Revolutionary War caused the early Congress many financial problems.

It is time we learn from history. The voters, who pay taxes, should take back their governments. How do the voters do this? By organizing groups and discussing what can be done? There is a need to let the officeholders know that now is the time for change. Numbers are always important facts to politicians. Letters, telephone calls, and e-mails all get their attention. These items transfer into votes. Letters to the newspaper editors inform others and get the attention of the media. The following paragraphs suggest material for voters to include in their efforts.

Today the Congress is composed of 535 individuals, the budget is so large the GAO cannot keep up with the spending, and the population is approaching four hundred million citizens in fifty states. Congressmen are more interested in reelection than governing the country. Lobbyists provide large sums of money for favors that are against the best interests of the citizens.

> The election of a president is more a popularity contest than a search for a well-qualified person. Candidates are chosen by a two-party system. About 60 percent of the country's population is active party members. The other 40 percent of the population generally votes *against* a candidate rather than voting *for* a candidate. Citizens are calling for change in the government.

> It is time for a Constitutional convention to examine and recommend a workable system for management and administration of the country. The number and size of the states need to be researched. The financial requirements and the tax base of the local, county, and state governments need study.

> Division of power between the states and the federal government requires serious examination. The organization, efficiency, and management of the federal government are of major concern. More concern should be given to tax revenue

and budget by the state and federal governments. The rapid rate of population growth also demands that changes in government occur as soon as possible.

According to the U.S. Bureau of the Census, the resident population of the United States as of February 16, 2010, at 19:12 UTC (EST+5) is projected to be 308,697,437. Because of the rapid grow in the population; estimates are available rather than solid data. The problems with the data from the census every ten years confirm this difficulty.

The factors used for the February 2010 estimates are as follows:

One birth every seven seconds

One death every eleven seconds

One international migrant (net) every thirty-four seconds

Net gain of one person every thirteen seconds

It is obvious that at this rate of growth, we will need changes now and changes in the future. Our government will always be dependent on the population and the budget amounts needed to provide services to the people.

The U.S. debt is frequently given as 1.3 trillion dollars, and the U.S. budget is near 3.6 trillion dollars. There is a rapid grow in both the debt and the budget. To pay the debt and support the budget requires approximately

$41,000 per person. That is about the average yearly income for families in the Tampa Bay area of Florida.

While a Constitutional Congress should reduce the size and the power of the federal government, the debt will remain. If the individual states provide funds for the federal budget, they should have control of the national budget. The national debt will remain as part of the individual states' responsibility. That U.S. debt is 1.3 trillion dollars. Most of the states now have an operational deficit.

After the reorganization brought about by the actions of the constitutional Congress, each state should have financial control of its affairs. The organization of the government and the method of taxation should rest with the state. The states could consider what method of taxation they should use. This could be an income tax, either graduated or flat tax, or it could be property-tax based. A value-added tax should also be considered.

A value-added tax is used by many countries. The budget of France is largely derived from a value-added tax. Tax is added for the purchase of raw materials and at each stage of manufacture. The taxes paid by corporations are passed on to the consumer by increasing the price of the end product. The tax is paid to the government at each stage of the manufacture. Like sales tax, this tax is a problem for the poor individual.

This control by states of government and taxation should provide greater fiscal responsibility. When the fifty states are reorganized into twenty states, each state will owe sixty-five billion dollars of the federal 1.3-trillion-dollar national debt. In addition, each state will owe the debt of the former states that joined the new state. The state debt will be about 1.5 times the average current state debt.

While these debt totals seem large, it should be remembered that the states will receive funds from the current federal accounts. The state taxpayers will have additional income from the removal of federal taxes. Further, the states will have considerable savings from current county and local operational funds.

The requirement that the states and the federal government operate on a balanced budget is extremely important. The requirement of a surplus sufficient to meet special needs is also important. This type of budgeting represents fiscal responsibility. One state should learn from the success of the other states. Currently, the federal government has completely lost all sense of fiscal responsibility. Between 2000 and 2009, we saw irresponsible spending that has led to the current major fiscal crises.

When Congress decided to use taxes as a way to bring about social changes—whereas taxes should be used to fund the government, we ceased to have fiscal responsibility. This type of taxation is mixing apples and oranges. We have seen the complications caused by such tax laws.

Living on borrowed money is not a suitable lifestyle for either the government or members of our society. The use of credit is necessary for some items with a high cost, but it should be remembered that interest adds to the cost of the item. Before buying on credit, the individual must consider the effects on their budget. They must know if income meets the expenses.

CHAPTER 6

THE COUNTRY'S NEED FOR FINANCIAL RESPONSIBILITY

Today the lack of financial responsibility at all levels of government and society is a problem. Money has value; and when money is invested, it makes money. Thus, money works. But when we live on borrowed money, the cost of living increases by the amount charged for interest on the borrowed money.

The government's administration has decided it can spend the country out of debt. The stimulus package has increased state spending and state debt. Thirty-five governors are suing the federal government because their actions have increased the states' budgets.

It appears that all levels of government and of our society have forgotten the value of money and its consequences. The requirement that state budgets have a surplus will provide income from the invested funds to the states. The surplus will also assure that programs can be properly funded.

This surplus requirement helps cover the ever-changing budget-to-income problems the governments will face. At a 7 percent interest rate, the investment doubles in ten years. Investment of the surplus will provide additional income to the individual state.

The members of our society and our governments need to learn the value of money. While money works and earns, today the Federal Reserve has placed such a low value on money, it is not worth what it should be. At one time, the 4 percent income on bank savings accounts was considered low. We need to get back to the days when a person was evaluated by the money he had in the bank—not as it is today, where he is evaluated on the basis of how much money the bank has in him.

The current credit score is a good example. When an individual has a high credit-to-debt ratio, they have a good credit score. This does not take into account the amount of money the individual has in the bank and other investments. If the individual has only one credit card and limited lines of credit, he can have money and investments but a lower credit score. This shows that Wall Street values borrowing over Main Street's value of saving.

Investments on Wall Street do not contribute to product production by industry. These investments help Wall Street but not Main Street. Investments in banks provide for consumer loans. This money is used to buy products. Product production requires employees.

Today we are struggling like the early Continental Congress, which struggled with the budget and how the country should be governed. The early Congress could not pay its debts from the Revolutionary War. The Iraq war and the long period of the Afghanistan war have contributed greatly to the current deficit.

But the Continental Congress had declared their independence from the British government and won the Revolutionary War. The Main Street citizens of today should take note of the Declaration of Independence and take control of the government "of the people."

The Declaration of Independence

1 When in the course of human events, it becomes necessary for people to dissolve the political bands which have connected them with another, and to assume among the powers of the earth, the separate and equal station to which the Laws of Nature and of Nature's God entitle them, a decent respect to the opinions of mankind requires that they should declare the causes which impel them to the separation.

2.1 We hold these truths to be self-evident, that all men are created equal, that they are endowed by their Creator with certain inalienable rights, that among these are life, liberty and the pursuit of happiness.

2.2 That to secure these rights, governments are instituted among men, deriving their just powers from the consent of the governed. That whenever any form of government becomes destructive of these ends, it is the right of the people to alter or abolish it, and to institute new government, laying its foundation on such principles and organizing its powers in such form, as to them shall seem most likely to effect their safety and happiness.

2.3 Prudence, indeed, will dictate that governments long established should not be changed for light and transient causes; and accordingly all experience hath shown, that mankind are more disposed to suffer, while evils are sufferable, than to right themselves by abolishing the forms to which they are accustomed.

2.4 But when a long train of abuses and usurpations, pursuing invariably the same object evinces a design to reduce them under absolute despotism, it is their right, it is their duty, to throw off such government, and to provide new guards for their future security.

2.5 Such has been the patient sufferance of these Colonies; and such is now the necessity which constrains them to alter their former systems of government. The history of the present King of Great Britain is a history of repeated injuries and

usurpations, all having in direct object
the establishment of an absolute tyranny
over these States. To prove this, let facts
be submitted to a candid world.

As we learn from our forefathers and the Declaration of Independence, it is well past the time for the people to recognize the problems with the current system of government and make real changes. Almost daily the media point out an individual involved in government who is very dissatisfied with our method of government. Recently several individuals have pointed to factors that have contributed to problems with our current method of government.

In addition to other factors, it is generally believed that the 2000 presidential election contributed to the political division in the country. Both the Democrats and the Republicans used every means to achieve victory. The two parties are more concerned with party victory than they are the welfare of the country. Congresspersons cannot compromise for fear of losing the backing of their party in the next election. The media today show this to be very true. Long-term members of Congress are losing the support of their parties and are not nominated for the general election. We are also seeing members of Congress who will not run for reelection because they are fed up with the dysfunctional Congress.

The evolution of media technology, which includes the 24/7 news cycle given us by Ted Turner, is blamed for much of the increase in partisan division. Advancement in science often has both good and bad effects. Internet blogging and its contribution to social networking has been a major factor in the Congressional bickering. The representatives must please their party to get a nomination for the next election.

Often the voters are blamed for the election of incompetent candidates. This does not seem to be the case. The candidates have good track records that show them to be competent. But after the election, they are placed in an incompetent and dysfunctional environment. Party politics and the aforementioned bickering have produced this dysfunctional Congress. The 2009 and 2010 congressional work on the health care bill is a very good example. This has been a good example of the role of the 24/7 news cycle and the Internet as ways to support partisan bickering.

Among the several congressmen who have decided not to be candidates for return to Congress are individuals from Indiana and Wisconsin. They have expressed dissatisfaction with Congress. Recently, three congressmen who seemed like ideal candidates, with sizeable war chests, would not run for reelection. These candidates were all seen as attractive and bright and moderate enough to attract voters from their states.

All of these candidates have stated they have had enough with the incompetence of the Congress. Several candidates from other states have recently announced that they will not run for reelection in 2010. They have all declared dissatisfaction with the lack of attempts by both parties to reach a consensus. It is no wonder Congress only has a 25 percent approval rating in the polls.

With our current Congress, where the members of both houses vote along party lines, it would be better if we elected one Republican and one Democrat and a few independent congressmen. The independent members would provide the swing votes. Just think how much money this would save the taxpayers. Limiting the congress to one house, the senate, should result in a better working environment. The powers of the federal government should be well defined. The states should have greater power.

REORGANIZING GOVERNMENT
WILL NOT BE AN EASY TASK

As stated before, many of these suggestions will seem very radical. It is easy for a society to become satisfied with the status quo. As Article 2.3 of the Declaration of Independence states, change should not be taken lightly. But it seems we have suffered enough. With governments on their present course, we may not have time for slow changes.

We have lived without major changes for many years. For one to accept things as they are and not think about the possibility for improvement in efficiency and effectiveness is understandable. Yes, the suggested changes are radical, but small changes will not work to correct the dysfunctional government and the waste of tax dollars that have grown over the past two hundred years. The twenty-first century has made this need for radical change more obvious.

Rearranging the powers and the budgets of the individual states will require considerable study. For example, how would the individual states handle education, health, and welfare? Providing a Social-Security income as a safety net for retired individuals would also be a major problem. Each individual state would have the power to establish its own tax structure. The income tax structure of the current federal government has caused many problems. The tax structure lost its primary purpose of funding the federal government and became a means to bring about social changes. This mixture of function has contributed to the difficulty with enforcement of tax laws.

The individual states might decide to have a value-added tax structure. This type of structure has been very successful in many countries. France reports that the paper documentation at each level of manufacture aids in the collection of the tax. With sales tax, there are frequent misstatements of the sales. Currently, a small percentage of the taxpayers pay the majority of the taxes.

Regardless of the tax structure chosen by an individual state, a yearly balanced budget should be required. The surplus fund could be used to operate the state in years when tax income was not sufficient to meet the state's needs. The surplus fund would be part of the new budget and need to be reestablished as rapidly as possible; this should not take more than four years. The surplus fund should eliminate deficit spending. If the taxpayers and voters demand this fiscal responsibility, the United States will return to its former world leadership position.

If individual retirement income became a state function and not a corporate function, an individual state retirement tax could be used to fund the program. When individuals move from job to job, their retirement income would be in the state-funded program. Collection of retirement funds should be similar to Social Security today.

If the retirement tax becomes a state function, the retirement income provided should be nearer the income needed for retirement. Today Social Security only places a safety net under retirement, and additional sources of income are required for retirement. While retirement income has been used to gain employee loyalty to the company, today companies are far less concerned about the welfare of their employees. This is obvious when one considers the number of jobs shipped overseas.

When individual states take over the function of our current Social Security program, the retirement age should include consideration of the average life expectancy. As the individual life expectancy increases, retirement age should increase. Since average life expectancy has been increasing, there have been many problems with funding of the current federal program that sets a retirement age unrelated to life expectancy.

We gather considerable data with the census every ten years. The data collected by the census should be used to solve government problems. For example, the data could be used to set state and county borders. While the example the author offered above suggested forty million for the region population, the population of current counties should be at least one hundred thousand.

Since individuals would pay into the retirement program all of their working lives, consideration should be given to early retirement as well as disability retirement. The individual needs an investment program that can support early retirement.

Income protection insurance protects individual income. The retirement funds in an individual account should be paid out as a life annuity with a twenty year guarantee period.

If the welfare programs are shifted to the individual states, funds now contained in federal programs should be shifted to the states. This would include the current Social Security funds and the funds that are owed to the Social Security program.

If health care insurance and insurance in general are under the control of the state governments, the decision making will be more under the control of the individual voters. The population of the citizen groups should make it easier to obtain a reasonable cost for the insurance. When individuals purchase insurance with tax dollars, control of cost is in the hands of the voters.

There should be natural disaster insurance to cover flooding, earthquakes, hurricanes, tornados, and other major disasters. As a federal program, the funds collected each year could be maintained nearer the yearly cost. The Federal Emergency Management Agency (FEMA) should remain a federal program. The Department of Homeland Security would be divided into federal functions and state functions.

In today's world, it is necessary to provide excellent security. While terrorism is a major concern, daily crimes in a community are a concern to the citizens. We read of murders in small cities as well as major metropolitan areas.

The following departments of government would be better served by moving them to state control: Department of the Interior, Department of Agriculture, Department of Commerce, Department of Labor, Department of Health and Human Services, Department of Housing and Urban Development, Department of Transportation, Department of Energy, and Department of Education. By moving these departments from federal control to individual state control, the decision making and funding would be near the citizens who would be affected by them.

Some points related to certain departments are very important and will take much consideration by the Constitutional convention. The Department of Commerce will need both federal and state considerations. Problems related to interstate commerce should remain a federal function.

The Department of Housing and Urban Development is a good example of the need for state control. Development should not be limited to urban areas. There are local and statewide concerns with development. States like California, Arizona, and Florida are examples where water supply is a major concern with development. Each state has its own set of problems where development is concerned.

The Department of Energy is another department where individual state concerns are important. The kind of energy development can be considerably different from state to state.

The development of additional nuclear energy is a good example of toxicity problems with disposal of the end products of use. We have seen this problem with nuclear energy; less recognized is the toxicity with the use of carbon fuels. The carbon dioxide produced by the use of gasoline and coal demonstrates another problem of adverse effects from the end products of use.

Shifting the problem from one area to another is not solving the problem. An automobile that uses electricity that is derived from a plant that uses fossil fuels is not solving the problem. Since oil is imported, the states and the federal government cannot control the price.

It is apparent that the work of a Constitutional Congress to solve these problems would be a massive task and would take time and effort. If the problem was shifted to the states, the task might be less complicated. Thus, for efficiency in government, we must rely on existing governments and the voters to bring about the changes.

CHAPTER 7

PAYING THE CURRENT FEDERAL DEBT WILL BE A MAJOR PROBLEM

The latest congressional budget estimates predict a 1.35-trillion-dollar deficit for this year as the economy tries to recover from the recession. The federal government is the largest employer. It is estimated that twenty-two million people are employed by the federal government. These workers have excellent benefits, including health care, sick leaves, and excellent retirement packages.

The dysfunction of the federal government is obvious. In general, the media believe that the federal government has become a very confusing system of government. Three major reasons are cited for the current dysfunctional government: (1) There are too many layers of government that are filled by political appointees. (2) The sunshine laws have failed to bring government into the open. (3) The shadow government is composed of a huge workforce, who often expresses dissatisfaction with their ability to get things done.

Several candidates for reelection have expressed their dissatisfaction with the operations of the Congress. Internet and newspaper reports have given fair warning about the crisis approaching in federal government. These warnings were ignored, especially during the early twenty-first century. We see the results every day. The federal government has too many decision makers and excessive central clearance. There are an excessive number of overseers. The overseers often have conflicting political agendas. There is also spending of tax dollars with little concern for efficiency.

With this confusing hierarchy, it is no wonder we have a budget deficit of 1.35 trillion dollars. Adding layers of hierarchy and increasing spending cannot be expected to correct the problems. They only add to the confusion of the hierarchy and increase government overhead cost.

While much has been said about the failures of the government, little has been done to bring about a change to a more workable government. If we wait for the people in office to bring about change that affects their jobs, we will wait a very long time for change and effective government.

CITIZENS CAN BRING ABOUT CHANGES THAT WILL LEAD TO A MORE EFFICIENT GOVERNMENT

While the freedoms of the Constitution are timeless, the wording expressing the freedoms requires clarification. There have been many instances in the history of the country where this lack of clarity of expression has led to problems. When we look at the history of oppression and slavery, we see a prime example. It was almost one hundred years after the words "All men are created equal" before Lincoln freed the slaves. During the Civil War, Lincoln removed habeas corpus. It was another hundred years before Congress passed the Civil Rights Act. Roosevelt placed Japanese, Germans, and Italians in prisoner-of-war camps without due process. More recently, there have been problems with wiretaps of citizens and problems with the rights of captured terrorists.

Recently the Supreme Court ruled that corporations could spend as much money as they wanted to support or trash a candidate. The ruling was related to freedom of speech. However, the ruling also gave a big advantage to special interest groups over citizens. It seems we have forgotten that our government is "of the people." Government "of the people" does not mean "government for special interests."

The amendments to the Constitution, generally referred to as the Bill of Rights, need some discussion when we are concerned with the law of the land. With the attorney general under the control of the president, it is easy for probable violations of the Constitution to occur.

The Bill of Rights needs to be more clearly worded. We need to define "terrorism" and "terrorist." Wars are no longer fought by men in uniform. Individuals captured during war are defined as combatants and tried in military courts. It would seem that terrorists and acts of terrorism should be defined as combatants and acts of war and be under the military courts. In wars we have had prisoners-of-war camps. We should develop such camps for terrorists and individuals accused of terrorism.

CHAPTER 8

CHANGES IN SOCIAL BEHAVIOR SHOULD SUPPORT CHANGES IN GOVERNMENTS

While considering changes in government, it is time to consider changes in our society. We must get back to faith in a vast majority of our citizens. The author is old enough to remember the post-World War II period. Considerable discussion of the time concerned divinity. It was said that society was becoming more divine. In the 1950s, you heard "corporate conscience" in conversations.

A course entitled "Principles and Problems of Secondary Education" pointed out that secondary education was to prepare students to become good citizens. One of the main principles was to teach that freedom required responsibility. Responsibility is lacking in society and government today.

We saw a major change in society in the 1960s. The individuals responsible for discipline in our society began calling for individual freedom, even at the expense of society.

Regardless of whether an individual believes in Christian teachings and the divine origins of these teachings, they represent some excellent guidance for the well-being of everyone. Martin Buber wrote that when one sees the words Jesus or Christ in the teaching, he should think "man"; when he hears "God," he should think "society"; and when he hears "the Trinity," he should think of the relationship between man and society.

After more than two thousand years of these teachings, one cannot say that society today is becoming more divine. Recent episodes of adultery are evidence for lack of respect for the teachings of the Ten Commandments. The deaths by gunshots and knife attacks on the streets each night are additional evidence of the lack of concern for others. So, as we have heard, society gets the government it deserves.

Almost daily we read of problems with the character of officeholders. It is impossible to tell whether these changes in morals are increasing dramatically or whether the advent of 24/7 news channels, blogs, and other Internet transfers of information have brought the problems to light. It is natural for copycats to try and act as the news has reported others have acted.

Our overcrowded prisons are a major problem. We need a court system that works more rapidly. We need to remove social psychopaths from society and keep them away from society.

Change is always difficult. When it comes to changing county and state borders, there will be a lot of opposition. Pride in one's state or county will cause resistance to changing borders. We have heard the saying, "Pride goes before a fall."

The recession of 2008 has caused many states to be in debt. The federal government has a tremendous debt. As of 2010, federal bonds are paying higher interest, because investors are becoming less sure the federal government will be able to pay off the bonds.

To continue the analogy of suggested changes to government from the corporate world, bankrupt corporations face reorganization. It would be wise to reorganize before becoming bankrupt. But even more important, reorganization to provide less overhead costs by downsizing state, county, and local governments will provide much-needed funds for the budgets of governments.

A budget must include payment on the principal and the interest on government loans. Falling behind on payments increases the fear of loss by investors. If the country intends to be competitive in the twenty-first century, we will need to have an efficient government structure. The needed increase in efficiency will allow the citizens to get more for their tax dollars.

Government and Society Are Living on Borrowed Money

While the dysfunctional federal government, with its inefficiency and a national debt of more than a trillion dollars is a major problem, state budget shortfalls of more than a billion dollars are common. Only six states did not have a shortfall in 2009.

Nineteen states had a shortfall of more than a billion dollars. The California shortfall was nineteen billion, and Illinois and New Jersey had shortfalls of more than four billion. The other sixteen states had shortfalls of one to two billion. Arizona's shortfall represents the largest percent of the operational budget. The shortfall was 24 percent of the state's budget.

The current 2010 budget problems are more disturbing. Only five states will not have a shortfall. The California shortfall will increase to almost forty-two billion dollars. Twenty-five of the other states project shortfalls of more than a billion dollars. As a percentage of the budget, the 2010 projections exceed the 2009 budget deficits.

These figures support the fact that all governments are continuing to outspend the income produced by their tax bases. Efforts to decrease overhead cost is absent. If this does not worry you, it should. What happens when individuals and corporations outspend their income? When they cannot borrow more money, they must file for bankruptcy.

The *Wall Street Journal* on January 2, 2010, identified federal stimulus funds as making the state budget situation worse. The stimulus funds were a one-time gift to the states. This gift was done by the federal government with borrowed money. Legislators enticed by the promise of federal money spent more money instead of adjusting budgets to declining revenue. Money was added for programs with yearly needs. The states will face increased budgets for important programs like K-12 education, higher education, child care, health and welfare benefits, and a large expansion of Medicaid to cover the health care of unemployed workers and single workers without children.

In 2011, when the federal funds run out, states will be stuck with one million more people on Medicaid with no money to pay for it. These facts show that current officeholders cannot function in an efficient and effective manner. Since the officeholders refuse to change, it is up to the citizens to demand mergers of governments and reductions in overhead spending.

If the news commentators on the various television networks would become better devil's advocates, the politicians would have to defend their positions on all the issues. A good devil's advocate would not let the politicians dance around the questions the way they do. The public needs answers now.

It's time to consider changes in our society and our government. The wording problems with the Bill of Rights pale when compared to the need for organization in the governments of the country. If more movements like the Tea Party and the Coffee Party support a Constitutional convention, we will have a Constitutional convention to bring about reorganization of federal, state, county, and local government.

These major organizational changes in governments will take a longer period of time than most taxpayers realize. The states and counties within a state need to undergo merger *now*. As reported earlier, the twenty-first century recession has caused trillions of dollars of loss in wealth, and individuals have accumulated a fourteen-trillion-dollar consumer debt.

With all but five of the fifty states reporting large shortfalls in their budgets, it is obvious that it is time states, counties, and local governments consider border changes that will provide an adequate tax base to pay off the governments' debt. Just as corporations need market share to match overhead, governments need tax base to match overhead.

The loss of wealth and the consumer debt will have a major effect on the ability of governments to raise sufficient tax revenue to operate governments. Tax increases will not help, but will hurt, the economy. Therefore, reduction in government overhead by mergers is the answer to current government financial problems.

Taxpayers and Voters Should Demand a Reduction in Government Overhead and More Efficient Government

Did you ever wonder why Philadelphia became the seat of the colonial and early federal government? Philadelphia burned with a high fever for separation from King George III. Freedom was the topic of conversations in coffee shops and other meeting places. Leaders like Franklin and Paine wrote pamphlets calling for independence. Thomas Paine's *Common Sense* was one of the pamphlets that gave great support to the Declaration of Independence and the Revolutionary War.

If the taxpayers and voters developed the same intestacy for change that increases tax savings that existed in Philadelphia for freedom, we would have centers that would bring about change.

Epilogue

Almost daily during the preparation of this manuscript, the author heard or read comments about our existing governments. Most of these comments were condemning government dysfunction. Budget and deficit problems were frequently discussed. TV commentators and their talking-head guests were more concerned with continuing political bickering than trying to provide solutions to the government's problems. We see and read mostly criticism without suggestions for improvement of efficiency or effectiveness.

We do not hear or read about the fact that corporate management and government management are similar. Corporations have deficits and budget problems. Especially lately, we hear of downsizing by a large number of corporations. As a result of the recession, we have seen mergers of several large companies. These mergers have resulted in layoffs of employees.

Government management takes a different approach to problem solving. Showing a lack of concern for deficit and budget problems, the various governments add another layer of government as a method of solving problems. These additional layers of government add confusion and dysfunction to the operations of governments.

While layoffs are not desirable, they are necessary. The proposed government layoffs will decrease government overhead spending. This decrease will put more money in the taxpayers' pockets and increase consumerism. This will result in an increase in corporate production and corporate jobs. It is better to have individuals contributing to the tax base than being a tax cost contributor.

As a result of the recession and the great loss of wealth, it is necessary that government management take lessons from corporate management. Just today the author read an article about the reduction in city and county tax base caused by the reduction in the value of real estate. Even with increases in tax rates it will be difficult for governments that rely on real estate taxes to balance their budgets.

If government were to use taxes properly to fund the government, we could reduce confusion in the tax codes. Taxes should not be used as a method to produce changes in social behavior. Funding government and changing social behavior are two different functions.

In addition, government should consider additional forms of taxes. We have had income tax, real estate tax, and sales tax long enough. Many nations use value-added taxes as their tax method. This method is used because it is easy to track the amount of taxes that should be paid. The value-added tax plan is much less confusing than the current federal tax laws.

The citizens of Philadelphia in the middle 1700s had a great desire to be free of the rule of King George III. Their efforts led to The Declaration of Independence and The Revolutionary War. It is time the voters and the taxpayers follow their example. Thus, the citizens will be free of the unnecessary dysfunctional governments. The tax payers and voters must take a greater interest in the finances of the government. Talk, blog, write, organize groups, use every method to bring about less government. Your actions can save tax dollars.